ANGER MANAGEMENT IN MARRIAGE

Ways to Control Your Emotions, Get Healed of Hurts & Respond to Offenses (Overcome Bad Temper)

By

Claire Robin

Other Books by the Same Author

I want to thank you for purchasing this book. After reading this book, dealing with anger, controlling other emotions and overcoming temper in your marriage and professional relationships will become easier. Below are other books that will also help in boosting intimacy and improving your marriage libido:

1. 100 Ways to Cultivate Intimacy in Your Marriage: How to Improve Communication, Build Trust and Rekindle Love

2. 200 Ways to Seduce Your Husband: How to Boost Your Marriage Libido and Actually Enjoy Sex: A Couple's Intimacy Guide

3. 232 Questions for Couples: Romantic Relationship Conversation Starters for

Connecting, Building Trust, and Emotional Intimacy

4. Communication in Marriage: How to Communicate Effectively With Your Spouse, Build Trust and Rekindle Love

Table of Contents

Introduction 5

Forms of Anger 13

Cure and Effect of Anger in Marriage Relationship 32

How to Tame Your Temper 52

How to Control Your Emotions 80

How to Benefit From Anger 104

Dealing with Angry Spouse 125

Conclusion 138

Other Books by the Same Author 140

Introduction

Anger in a relationship is the worst form of emotion often directed to our loved ones. This intense emotional response is often strong and most people don't have an actual control of its occurrence. In a relationship, anger occurs when a partner feels threatened or hurt by the other. Sometimes anger transpires during a conversation when a person feels accused or threatened by a particular phrase.

Even though most perceived threats are not threats at all, it is very important that an individual is able to manage his or her own anger. In relationships, personal boundaries are very important. These personal boundaries become even more important in committed relationships, where an individual will need a particular space, away from the significant other. A partner constantly crossing a set boundary is ultimately violating your personal privacy and the only emotion relevant as a response is the anger emotion.

Most of the times, couples get back to each other by doing something even worst in order to make the other person feel the same emotion. On the other hand, some will just react with rage, and yelling, or even resort to physical violence as an expression of the anger emotion.

The limitation of anger control depends on the amount of pressure felt at a particular time. Calmness could be ultimately determined by the amount of anger pressure felt at this period of time. The willpower to remain calm and in control of the situation is only limited to time.

People tend to label anger as a common emotion that has to be dealt with by constant suppression, but the effect of anger on your body system makes it very crucial to master the methods of channeling the emotion towards something even better than explosiveness.

Also, anger has a direct effect on your physical and mental health. Adrenaline level is evidently increased when anger is felt, blood pressure is elevated, and heart rate consequently increases. The flight response as a result of anger provides the foremost and immediate reaction or first aid to calm the brain down. At times, sadness, hurt and fear are the underlying elements of anger. In fact, some people use anger to hide such emotions in an attempt to make people think they are strong and not sad, hurt or fearful.

The instant behavior to protect your emotions or ego from the external sources of psychological, cognitive and behavioral threats can be portrayed by anger. This is because your action is more conscious, even as you fight a particular feeling using another.

It is important in a relationship, to know when your partner is angry and how to show that you are angry without the need to yell or resort to violence. Apart from aggression, you can read anger emotions through mental responses, body language and most of all, facial expressions. These expressions could happen immediately at an occurrence of an incident that provokes someone's emotions, or intermittently as elements of anger are built up a step at a time.

These expressions are expressed first before any other physical activity is being taken against the adversary. So, it is important to be aware of these expressions, to feel and control your anger, and to also act against the wrath of another person when they are angry at you.

Anger management is a two-way street; you need to understand anger both in your person and in other individuals. Also, it is of the essence to realize that anger can take away your rational judgment, your observatory objectives and also the capacity to monitor behavior or reactions properly; thus not every anger reaction can be justified even when you are truly hurt by the other person.

Feeling angry or reacting as a result of anger does not determine your level of maturity. Everybody can be angry, but the differences between saving your relationship and sabotaging the opportunity for change is how you control this emotion.

In fact, for your relationship to survive, you need to actualize your anger triggers and make them known, so they can both be avoided and managed. You need to understand exactly what you do that make other people feel hurt or threatened, and what other people do capable of making you feel threatened or hurt.

On the other hand, anger is important in a relationship as a form of expression, to show exactly how you feel about something being done wrong. Corrective actions are best mobilized through the expression of anger. In professional relationships, sometimes your employees need to be afraid of your rage in order to perform their work faster with better focus.

For your partner to be diligent and not to take what you say for granted, they must be afraid of your reaction at some point.

Nevertheless, anger emotion or the expression of anger is not the only option for controlling people or making them do what you want. We shall discuss alternative emotions further in this book.

If anger is not controlled, the negative impact is almost devastating and can overshadow all the assumed positive benefits. Essentially, people find it hard to relate or to stay around an individual that resort to the expression of anger in getting things done. For your social benefit, anger management should be patronized as much as possible.

Furthermore, anger can cause emotional trauma when control is absent. Anger suppression must be tactical in order to make sure you provide for emotional balance and impulse control. Some tactics in suppressing anger may cause more anger since the emotion can be confined in one place, which outburst could be unpredictable. It is important to also realize when a person is showcasing anger just to get a social recognition or to influence people.

Forms of Anger

Psychologically, three forms of anger are recognized:

Dispositional anger

Deliberate anger

And sudden anger

Dispositional anger is a form of anger based on primary cognitions and instincts. This form of anger does not depend on the characteristic of the external source of behavior, but the person's instincts. In the physical, it is often showcased as churlishness, sullenness, and irritability.

Deliberate anger is basically episodic and is characterized by the perception of threats or harm deliberately directed unto the individual. For example, the deliberate anger is the form of emotion felt when you feel like you are deliberately being treated unfairly by someone.

Sudden anger involves protection of self from harmful emotions or external sources of hurt or intimidation. The self-preserving action is almost impulsive and this is common when an individual feels the need to be liberated from an emotional trap or torment.

In a relationship it is only important to understand the characteristics of anger and the role they play in determining the direction of your emotions, commitment level, and intimate satisfaction.

Passive Relational Anger

In a relationship, passive anger is expressed in different ways. In order to manage anger effectively you need to understand these expressions;

Constantly blaming yourself

The extent of passivity is when you constantly blame yourself of the wrongdoings of another party, even when you've been doing everything right. It is important that you recognize self-blame as a passive anger emotion, and take the time to identify the sources of such anger. When you find yourself apologizing even when you did everything right, there might be some form of passive anger that needs be taken care of.

Becoming secretive

Since passiveness is all about drawing less attention to yourself, you may want to show your anger but in the absence of the people, you are angry with. Behaviors associated to the secret passivity includes stealing, complains, gossiping, muttering and most importantly, silent treatment. In this case, you are recommended to head for the issue that is causing the behaviors instead of focusing on the hurt or the anger that is planted within your mind.

Mental manipulations

People with passive anger tend to criticize people and at the same time be on their side. On the other hand, they are good at causing rage, as they stay calm and watch you overreact. These people also have anger but don't have the reasonable platform or guts to showcase their emotions.

The characteristics associated with these form of anger include, negative conveyance of feelings, sexual provocation, fake illness, and blackmailing, often pointed to the emotions. Relationships are easily sabotaged with this form of anger, and the person in question may end up lonely since no one can trust them with their emotions.

Obsession

As a result of an underlying anger, this person will feel the need to be perfect in some things not necessarily relevant or important to the relationship. In the place of work, a boss with passive anger may need all the jobs done fast and perfectly all the time. Even though such ethic seems to align with the conventional cooperativeness, an individual may be stuck in seeking for perfection in a particular work department, while other parts of the work suffer deprivation. Other characteristics include obsession to a good diet, organic foods, over-cleanliness or constantly correcting mistakes in others.

Defeatism

This involves setting a goal purposefully to fail with other people. This form of behavior is almost sadistic but also involves self-sabotage tendency, where the individual may not care if they fail, inasmuch as other people are going to fail with them. It is also characterized by the tendency to focus on unimportant details in relationship or work process while leaving the important ones to rot. When it comes to teamwork, this person may deliberately choose the wrong people or people with known weaknesses, so the expectancy of certain failures becomes definite.

Evasiveness

This person may not be necessarily the cause of crisis but whenever his or her input is needed for a solution to stick, they will never be found handy. They easily turn their backs on instant responsibility or try to play hide and seek at the time they are really needed to perform a particular task. This form of passive anger is also associated with lack of responsibility or shying away from responsibility in an attempt to send a message about a certain feeling. Although this reaction can be rarely perceived as a message, the individuals often achieve satisfaction.

Dispassion anger

This form of passive anger is characterized by consistent neutrality to situations. The person may look unconcerned even in situations they are practically needed to show some concern. They show no feeling of any kind even during an emotional moment. Instead, they pursue exclusively something that has to do with the intellects in order to avoid other people.

The person in question can easily objectify other individuals while giving too much attention to objects, machines or devices. In the internet age, individuals with such anger tend to focus on social media in an attempt to avoid real interaction. Other characteristics of such passivity are oversleeping and substance abuse.

Aggressive Anger

Retaliation

This form of aggressive anger is characterized by personal vengeance. It is one of the worst forms of aggressive anger often has no limitation on the form of action being taken just to feed the negative emotion. Importantly, retaliation or retribution does not seek justice; it seeks to destroy to an extent of satisfaction. In this case, most vengeance ends up in regrets and the reduction of sanity. The overly punitive characteristic is almost labeled more dangerous than actual evil.

Unpredictable explosion

This person may explode unpredictably even over simple issues. Their argument is usually illogical; basically focused on satisfying the emotions instead of the essence of the particular fact being discussed. The use of drugs and alcohol is common among the people dealing with explosive anger.

Bar fights may be common, even as they expose themselves to more harm and danger than they can handle. Since the emotions have little or no control, their loved ones are also unsafe. Also, this person may attack the other party without notice over things that happened in the past. As a result, frustration is built up and in the long run, depression.

Constantly blaming others

This person will make a vivid mistake but still stand to blame others for the same mistakes. Accusations about facts, theories and the failure of a work process are common, and the next person is the one to take all the heat. If they don't feel good about something, they tend to ask people uncomfortable questions instead of first checking on their activities, choices and even perceptions.

Making involuntary threats in order to intimidate people

Such aggressive anger resorts to actions not directly aimed at harming people but to show the signs of harm capability. They are mostly characterized by simple to even extreme threats. Behaviors might be to slam doors, rage driving, wearing aggressive tattoos, pretending to be friends with thugs, change in walking posture, deliberately coming late when they promised to be earlier, and most of all, telling the subject that they are capable of destroying a property or even hurting a loved one if their demands for emotional fulfillment are not met.

Selfish acts

This is common among individuals with aggressive anger personality, and it is characterized by consistently making sure that other people don't get what you get. It's the worst form of self-centeredness, where an individual can use the bridge, and then burn it, in an attempt to prevent other people from reaching the same destination. Even if they are asked to help, they straightforwardly decline such request and may not even think twice about it.

Manic behavior

These behaviors are common and actually obvious when someone is angry; involves evident recklessness, becoming careless with words, and even when driving.

Hurtful violence

Firstly, hurtful violence can be expressed by labeling other individuals; blaming other people for one's wrongdoings; making sure other people know that you are ignoring their feelings; making people feel trashed by manipulating their confidence. It also includes verbal abuse as a form of communication with underserved people; sexual abuse, and violence. The aim, in this case, is to derive satisfaction in hurting other people, as an attempt to deal with anger.

Exempt grandiosity

This is characterized by using the opposites of known methods of solving a problem. The individual may close down on people when the only solution to a problem is a discussion. The demand for attention at this time is so high, even though the individual may shy away from simple delegations. When this anger becomes long-term, distrust is built and isolation from social activities.

Becoming an agent of destruction

Just like the other obvious signs, this also involves drugs or alcohol abuse, deliberate destruction of someone else's self-esteem, feigning emotional attacks, and even attacking innocent animals. It is also characterized by intentional vandalism, even of possessions that have personal values to the person.

The bully agent

In this case, the person maybe quick in figuring out the weak side of people and tend to wok right through it. Shouting and yelling is common in this case. The individual may also resort to threats and emotional persecution often initialized using verbal abuse.

Assertive Anger

Constant sternness

This involves expressing blatant disapproval when another person misbehaves. Assertive anger does not involve any violent physical action, but the sternness and restriction in principle, even as voice coordination is uncontrolled. Anger caused by disappointment is often expressed assertively either to correct, convey faults or just to express how one feels.

Assertiveness is an important aspect of a committed relationship but self-expression in anger is discouraged due to the need to reduce the chances of arguments and to achieve a reasonable aim whenever you are discussing intimate issues with your partner.

Punishment

The person in question may express his anger through punishing the person at fault. This type of expression is almost healthy inasmuch as it is regulated. The form of punishment should be acceptable and should not pose risk to the life or health of the individual. The punishing expression of assertive anger is common among parents, where they punish kids when they do wrong by limiting the kids' access to pleasure or social life. These pleasures may include video games, going out with their friends, movie time, etc. These punishments are often temporary.

Blame and justification

This type of assertive expression of anger should be employed in both personal and business relationships to maintain orderliness, even as you frown upon the wrong deeds of others. Discipline is very important in cultivating a healthy relationship, so justified blaming or scolding is very important to express the need for such discipline on employees, loved ones, kids and even friends.

The importance of voting out all the forms of anger is to be able to actualize exactly the kind of expression common to your anger. Once you become aware of your angry expressions, managing anger will become a lot easier. The amount of time needed to achieve the self-discipline and commitment often needed to bring about change in the way you control emotions will be less.

Also, it is important that you understand the forms of anger in order to know exactly when a partner is angry and when he or she is expressing the anger wrongly. In this case, your job should be to indicate other ways your spouse could express their anger without the need to break things or be reckless about things that really matter to them or the relationship as a whole.

Anger management brilliancy is crucial for every relationship to thrive. Although it will take longer for you to recognize when you have reached a limit of a reasonable reaction to the anger emotion, it is important to begin mastering all details, in order to reach a reasonable level of awareness.

Marriage communication could be made easier once anger expression during a discussion is limited. Even though some anger expressions are morally and practically correct, anger management demands that you know when to express your anger and when not to sabotage a particular value just because you need to express the emotion.

Cure and Effect of Anger in Marriage Relationship

"Marriage is an institution where everything is faced the way it is."

The fantasy or assumptions of wild romance and perfection of life is forgotten, and replaced by responsibilities; to care about this one person regardless of the emotions involved. It is an obligation that you understand this person fully, in order to avoid hurt and to make sure their needs are being met.

Unlike your early stage of dating where every issue or negative vibe could be solved with a kiss, marriage demands more than physical touch in bringing a reasonable end to a problem. Even though the level of challenges couples pass through solely depends on circumstances and the personality traits possessed by both individuals, the crisis is common even among the most compatible partners.

Differences have to be worked out, and challenges have to be dealt with in the first 12 to 20 years of marriage. It is important to note that the success of your marriage also depends on the willingness to work your differences out. Giving up on the side of any of the couples often results in divorce or endless unhappiness and dissatisfaction.

These are the causes of anger emotions in marriage, and ultimately why most marriages don't work out. Keep in mind all the details in order to pick one at a time as you explore your marriage intimacy to the utmost.

When Needs Are Belittled

Intimate relationship demands that you understand the need of your man or woman. Passive anger is the worst kind of anger in the history of marriage. It is silent and only eats up the core of your relationship. Before you even realize, you are sitting on an empty ball, only to collapse, leaving you sinking in the deep. Anger and resentment work hand in hand, and it is your responsibility to avoid the occurrence of both.

The needs of men: There is nothing a man needs than encouragement that comes as a form of affirmation; and sex that comes as an obligation to fulfill the need for sexual intimacy. As a wife, sex and affirmation should be the two words you don't play with, as much as you want to avoid the building up of anger or resentment in your husband. The lack of the two may not directly cause outrage but they surely play important roles in making your husband feel like you are being inconsiderate, as a result, resort to being the same thing. Thus, any other gesture might not be perceived with value.

The needs of women: A typical woman needs the random act of kindness, and unfortunately, most men ignore this need. Secondly, she needs your appreciation. Thirdly, and most importantly, she needs you to listen. Depriving your wife one of these things will render your wife unhappy or dissatisfied with any other gesture you make.

It is not for a woman to decide what she wants, it is nature that decided long ago that women should need to be heard, appreciated and also get attention from their significant other. It is written in the *Humanity Bible* that any woman deprived of such need may not be happy regardless of her achievements or other things she could get from her spouse.

All these needs are relevant to marriage or any committed relationship. Just the way you cannot deprive garden-plant water, you cannot deprive your partner such needs. Passive or assertive anger usually occurs as a result of such deprivation. Importantly, the passion of relationship easily withers in the absence of such nourishment. The less important you take them, the more they become important to the life of your marriage as a whole.

This all comes down to the human need for validation. Even the people that don't seem to care about validation in the outside world are easily affected by the fact whether they are getting validation from their spouses or not. Anger begins to build up when partners begin to use their lack of satisfaction to blame one another anytime they get the opportunity.

The emphasis provided creates the definiteness of the feelings being engineered as a result of the unmet need. Real intimacy or the possibility of growth practically vanishes. Hope on things that matter even in the place of work or career may begin to fade. Instead of seeing the world as it is, the partner affected will begin to feel the hole of emptiness grow even deeper.

More anger can be cultivated in cases where spouses withhold a certain need as a form of punishment. For example, withholding sex because your partner doesn't meet up with time, without actually discussing facts, may give him ideas to seek other alternatives for satisfaction.

Closing down on your wife just because you want her to be more attentive may bring about more distance when there's no actual demand for attentiveness. Whenever you feel the need to punish your partner, make sure you warn them of your actions before proceeding, so they will have the chance to change for good and to also make some demands that will help in his or her transformation.

The Righteousness Drive

"When you assume you are right about everything you think of, even before discussing it with your spouse; when you think the decision you make is perfect and final even when your spouse may disagree; and during discussion, when you demand that your spouse should just shut up and listen because you are saying the right thing."

Marriage relationship demands that the two should be treated as equals and no opinion should be better than the other. Consistently making your spouse feel like they are on the wrong side or depriving them a chance for the contribution they need to make on the things that actually concern them may result in anger.

Taking another route just because you want to assume some amount of power or control will only result in rebellion, which is often accompanied by anger. Reasonability should be defined by the amount of time you are willing to spend in making sense of things that bother your relationship.

Even when you are sure about making sense in everything, reasonability demands that your spouse should be involved in validating your opinions or suggestions before any action is taken.

Again, assumptions should be avoided in actualizing right or wrong when it comes to the marriage relationship. Your point of view is only right when it applies to you personally as a person. The value of your perceptions only thrives as long as your spouse gets to chip in.

In the case where you negotiate with your spouse on everything but decide to do it on your own, you should be expecting your spouse to also cultivate such habit. On the other hand, it's your responsibility to allow your spouse to make decisions that concern them without coming with your grand suggestion. It is one thing to do things without putting your spouse into consideration; it is another to drive your spouse crazy by becoming nosy in their affairs.

If you are on the other side of the picture, where you don't get to choose or make suggestions, it is best you begin to discuss the particular issue with your partner. If your spouse can't listen to you even during the polite discussion, marriage counseling sessions might be your best option, to get someone to tell him or her of the need to slow down and allow you to make inputs as well.

When Your Anger Or Pain Cannot Be Controlled...

Anger is the easiest element that can elevate anger. The control you have for present emotions and pains will determine how you are being perceived even as you take responsibilities. Anger is not just about regular explosion, violence or yelling; it is also about pretention.

People with a chronic form of anger tend to pretend that everything is fine just to avoid discussing the issue with their significant other. Although peace may reign for some time when you avoid confrontations, the pain and frustration as a result of continuous suppression might be detrimental to your actual productivity in the relationship.

Anger, in this case, becomes the silent killer of the affection you have for your spouse. Honesty is hard to practice when you don't want to look like the breaker of peace in your marriage. While you keep dying on the inside, your spouse may think that your lack of affection is a choice, and they may follow suit, to become even worse in giving you the right attention, often ignoring your needs for intimacy.

Anger as a whole may continue to grow in this occasion, and the only breaker is when you decide to talk things through and admit to yourselves the feelings that have been long suppressed.

Pain is the second thing that should be considered when it comes to emotional suppression. Your pains should come to life, even as you express them to your spouse. It is recommended that your pains and disappointments should be practically expressed immediately as they are felt; never to go to bed without discussing the bad feeling you have about an issue.

This will, in turn, open a door for constant communication of feelings between you and your partner, and you will ultimately discover effective ways to solve emotional problems.

Cooling off is important, and ignoring some pains can be healthy to some extent. But you don't have to pretend everything is fine when consciously you can still feel the pain of deprivation or betrayal. The importance of an issue at some point is only determined by the intention of its occurrence. You are to determine whether the issue occurred mistakenly, or whether it is turning into a particular habit in your marriage relationship.

Furthermore, suppression of anger or exposing yourself to circumstances that make you angry will make you even angry at yourself. At some point, you should believe that you don't deserve to be angry. But you need to be realistic about the underlying emotions that might trigger the emotions of anger.

So, instead of locking your dispositions in some narrow pipe of rational deliberation, allow yourself to feel everything, to act according to feelings and to tell people that contribute to your hurt that you are truly affected.

Imagine a circumstance where you don't want to feel angry so you don't show your anger, and your spouse shows his or her anger, and you are forced to feel bad about it. In this case, you are going to work really hard in making sure you get rid of their pains while your pains remain consistent, and even stimulated due to the self-betrayal.

Better yet, imagine a scenario where you have to fake orgasms or give silent treatments just because you feel the need to keep your partner feel validated even when they are not doing really well. And because you don't want to look like the only complainer, this keeps going for a very long time.

Ironically, the moment you think you are the one that always complains, believe in the fact that you are the only one who is not actually complaining. Do not be afraid to express your emotions even if you are the only person that wants improvement in the relationship.

Faking headaches just because the sex is bad and trying to be passive about it may not solve your passive anger problem. The best way to manage this type of anger is to make time to actually communicate the problem with your spouse.

If you need to change positions, or even include dirty talks when having sex; discuss it with your spouse. But then, you need to make sure that all other sources or causes of resentment are being dealt with altogether. The importance of peace is not about keeping it; it is also about making it.

When You Are Always a Victim

Every conflict in marriage relationship must involve a victim. For example, you might be the perfect spouse that does everything right and according to the books, but surprisingly; your spouse needs to find a way of making your effort look useless, or better yet, purposely doing things that will help undermine your effort.

In this case, it is easy to feel like your spouse doesn't think you exist anymore when you are taken for granted. Also, your spouse never considers your effort and gets insensitive about issues around the home. The underestimation and over-indulging become a bigger problem when you don't protest or ask for anything. They may even begin to feel like you are no more relevant in the marriage relationship as a whole.

Your forgiveness becomes too much even when they are unfaithful and unapologetic. Your anger may not mean anything to them because you made yourself passive in the relationship.

Even if the relationship ends, you will still feel like you've been cheated and will carry the anger and resentment along for a very long time.

The best thing to do is to find a safe ground where you can actualize on all the feelings you are feeling and make sure that you construct ways by which those feelings can be expressed.

When You Can't Relate Well With the Relatives

Conventionally, marriage longevity is determined by how well you are able to get along with your in-laws. If you have to take separate sides in making choices or determining the future of your marriage, it is apparent that your in-laws will have more influence on your spouse than you do.

Having continuous issues with your in-laws may render you unhappy, and when your spouse doesn't take your side, you will end up angry and dissatisfied. The stronger the bond you have with your in-laws, the better you do in maintaining a happy long-term relationship.

According to researchers, men who get along with their in-laws have greater chances of maintaining a happy marriage than women who get along with their in-laws. When a woman consistently listens to her in-laws, she easily makes the wrong choices, gets frustrated, and starts hating everyone and ultimately complications will begin to transpire in her relationship with the husband.

It is very important as a woman that you regulate the way you relate with your in-laws even as you pursue a long happy marriage. You are free to say NO to demands, and YES to the things you are comfortable with. It is your job to save yourself from anger emotions that might lead to an outburst, destroying an essential part of your relationship; respect. Let constant assertiveness be acknowledged, and speak more with your spouse about your feelings, so you could get the needed support when dealing with outside parties.

How to Tame Your Temper

Putting aside theories for a while taming, let's look at the simple, less scientific ways to tame your anger.

Remember, the more you interact with people socially, the more you will need a particular control of sudden pressures even when they come as positive emotions. Anger, most especially most be tamed without the need to feel like you are doing a heavy job. The quality of relationships you have will ultimately depend on your ability to manage anger. And, managing anger means knowing how to express it and when to suppress it.

Identify Your Bullet Solutions

Simply, try as much as possible to distract yourself from the details that made you angry and focus on the possible solutions that will bring an end to the negative circumstance. In this case, you need to wear the shoe of a leader. You need to be the problem solver instead of the complainer.

Self-control is the most important trait you need in order to make this possible. You need to put yourself in the position of responsibility, with the acknowledgment that what you do or say will affect everything that goes around in the environment.

For example, instead of focusing on the mess your partner made in the bedroom by leaving everything out of place, get out, close the door and get some fresh air. Use the time to figure out both the instantaneous solution to the problem and the permanent solution which has to do with confronting your husband about change in attitude or habit.

During the confrontation, you are free to describe how angry and disappointed you are. For a change, using the phrase "I feel disappointed" instead of "I feel angry" will help your discussion last longer and your partner will feel the need to change. Nobody wants to be a disappointment.

If your husband is always late for the dinner, learn to have the meal on your own or schedule a late meal in order to fill the space. What is the possible reason for his lateness? Is it work? Whatever the reason, you need to work together into finding a reasonable compromise even as you grow to fit into different schedules together.

Continuous reaction to wrongs or negativity may not fix the problem. In fact, anger outbursts reduce your chances of fixing things, since your partner may only do things when they are afraid that you will yell, not because they understand how important that thing is to you.

Take a Timeout

Sometimes you need to take a break from marriage, kids, work, in fact even your spouse. You need to create a space for yourself where everything will be seen as it is. You need to let go of control and allow things to flow at their natural pace. In-between house chores, take a timeout to watch an episode of a TV show.

During work hours, use the happy hour to actually have fun and forget about the pile of work waiting for you in the office. Learn to manage your time a day at a time, and one moment for every task. Do not take every responsibility, even if you are in the right position to handle them.

Give yourself unplanned breaks between tasks whenever you feel pressured or stressed.

Sometimes you tend to feel irritated for no reason and anybody close to you has no choice but to take the heat. Realize the underlying effects of your anger and discuss it with your partner. If you need a week break from the responsibilities at home, ask for that.

If you want to go out on a crazy adventure in order to figure yourself out, make sure you make time for that. If you need to cry out or shout about something, make a time to shout and even cry about anything. Make sure that all the crazy ideas about putting yourself in order are being met.

Exercise for a While

Do not remain stagnant and expect a healthy mental synchronization. You might be mentally boxed without realizing it. Lack of flexible interpretation of situations may have a strong effect on the way you handle pressure and stress as a whole. Exercises provide the flexibility to reduce stress and to also allow for better mental coordination.

Just a simple walk or run might change the way you perceive things, calm yourself down and even figure out a final solution to a problem. Physical activities like sports are very important in making sure that you remain healthy even as you seek improvement. Involve in sports games that will improve your mood and patience with people, thus finding a balance between following principles and letting things progress in their natural forms.

Make sure you give this pleasure to your person, and never forget that your mental and physical health matters, even as you are responsible for the growth of your relationship.

The Calm Expression of Anger

Become assertive in expressing your anger to the people in question. But then, you don't need to express your anger immediately. Wait for your emotions to subside, then spit out your feelings and let them know how affected you are by their actions.

Your expression doesn't have to be all about confrontation, just make sure you express your frustration in a way the person will recognize the importance of not repeating the same action in the future. Make yourself clear as you suggest a better way of treatment or conduct, which should be demonstrated directly to the person.

This shows that you don't only value your emotions, but you know exactly how you want to be treated and you are assertive enough to outline your demands. In all these, you don't need to try to control the people in question, all that matters is the expression, and then you let go.

Remember, your calmness is almost as important as the control you have over situations. If you fail to be calm on some issues, you may not be able to achieve control. In some cases, when people do something intentionally to make you angry, responding with rage is only going to make them feel satisfied and fulfilled. Deprive them the show, and instead put them on the show by assuming control of the situation.

Thoughts Should Come First

"Just the way you were thought social education; think before you speak. It is that simple."

By now you should understand that anger blocks the tendency of all rationality; the thought capacity is being reduced and the conscious steps to feel the need to apply rational thinking in handling situations. Emotional intelligence demands that you allow your rationality to determine the effect of an external force, therefore processing all the details that matters, starting from the reasons for their actions, why you are affected and the best way to handle the situation to ensure that you don't lose control.

Emotional intelligence is all about control and communicating with the emotions of other people while still putting your emotions into consideration. The aim here is to avoid doing or saying something that will cause regret in the long run, even immediately. Let your expression be as constructive as possible, even as you hold on to the control.

So, counting 1 to 15 before exploding is very important when it comes to outrage. After counting you will realize that what you were about to do or say before you started counting are not even worth it; so you will have the chance to instead say something more effective.

On the other hand, also allow other people to gather their thoughts and talk only when they have actualized on the best things to say. Do not pressure them to start talking, thus you will be able to achieve an actual solution to the given problem. It is important to tell the other person to calm down politely so that they don't escalate or make a scene.

Remember Your Relaxation Techniques

There are many forms of relaxations that might actually help you in taming your anger. The most important ones are the ones you have used before and they worked for you. Some people play musical instruments to calm down, some choose deep breathing exercises, and some use mantras while others prefer creative visualization. Whatever the effective form of relaxation, make sure you use it often in order to achieve a relaxed mind whenever you are faced with a reason to be angry or better before you go out to a place where there is a tendency of anger.

Over the past decade, Yoga has been extremely effective in helping individuals keep their composure. The exercise induces a stronger focus on individuals. When this focus is directed to inner peace, individuals tend to be flamboyant and uneasily altered by external sources of negativity.

Other people resort to eating chocolate or taking a cup of coffee, just to keep the composure in check. Evidently, you are to focus on the things you do that make you feel some amount of ecstasy. Black chocolate has been discovered to improve mental energy, which means the ability to maintain composure even in the midst of adversaries.

Do Not Forget Your Sense of Humor

The best way to release tension between people evidently hating on each other is the use of humor. Sometimes in the marriage relationship, couples tend to feel really irritated by the presence of each other, especially when some issue has been raised that poses a threat to the relationship. When your partner is struggling to control his or her temper, go nuts with your sense of humor and get a good laugh.

In this case, your partner will open up even more, and you will both have chances, to be honest with yourselves about the issues you have to deal with in your marriage relationship. It is important that you diffuse this tension in order to win the heart of your partner once again. Humor, even when you are alone, can help you feel better about yourself, and you will begin to think clearly about the things that are making you angry.

Your thoughts will become rational and relevant to the actual possibilities of solutions. You will have a clear picture of how things should go, even as you maintain control of yourself, and have a really constructive way to express your feelings. Do not mistake sarcasm to humor or humor to sarcasm. It is very important that you avoid sarcasm when your partner is clearly angry in order to avoid further escalation of emotions. Sarcasm should only be used when your partner is in a good mood, or you don't use it at all.

When Forgiveness Could Work

"Actually, forgiveness could work in bringing about positivity even in the worst moments."

If you could just forgive this person, you will achieve the power to do even better things. Forgiveness is a symbol of maturity and control, where a person is perceived to have control over negative emotions by allowing positive feelings to determine his or her words and actions. Only the strong forgive, and your strength is clearly not a weakness, even as your partner acknowledges the fact that you know exactly when they don't deserve what they are getting.

The relationship can be strengthened by the simple act of forgiveness. It is very important to make sure the value of that forgiveness is maintained by reminding your partner constantly that the actions which are being forgiven are not to repeat themselves, regardless of the circumstance.

Leverage the "I" statement

I don't want to feel angry again…

I feel disappointed…

I don't like the way…

I realize that you don't …

I am upset that you…

Instead of;

You make me feel disappointed…

You are responsible for all of this…

You are to be blamed that…

You never take the chance to…etc.

The aim is to avoid placing blames on your partner while you give them time and space to actually recognize their faults. Criticism will bring about defensiveness, and in the end, you might end up not achieving anything from the discussion. It is important therefore that you express yourself based on how you feel, not what is being done. And even if you want to state what is being done wrong, you can be less accusative.

Try as much as possible to reduce tension even as you work on your tone of expression. Whenever you feel like you are getting emotional and may harm the calmness of the moment, pause and allow things to go first. So, it is important to choose a place and time where your emotions cannot be altered, and if they do, you cannot lose your balance, so that all other things will remain under control. Only have two words on your mind when resolving an issue with your partner; being **specific** and **respectful**. Finding solution becomes easier when the two traits are maintained.

Face Your Fears of Rejection

It is easier to tell when you feel like you are being ignored than to admit that you feel insecure. It's natural to feel like your partner will reject your endeavors or effort in becoming a better person or even, doing things differently than before. It is very important that you stop driving yourself crazy by diverting your focus from the fear and aligning yourself to the adventure experience involved in realizing your fault and getting better along the way.

Marriage is an institution of growth and improvement; you should make it clear to your spouse that it is okay if they make mistakes, inasmuch as they will accept correction. In turn, you can also tell them to correct you anytime they feel like you are doing something wrong. Defenselessness should not necessarily mean resisting corrections; you should use the emotion as a vehicle for change, where the energy will be directed to the need for satisfaction when something is done actually right.

Most couples choose the easier path, which is: being angry with their partners. Admitting to mistakes and facing your fear of rejection may not be easy, but the difference will remain significant in the long run. Also, try and see the consequences of angry reaction to the state of your relationship in order to create more reasons not to resort to anger when you feel vulnerable. Just the way you cannot scream at a coworker at work because you don't want to get fired, you don't need to scream at your spouse since he or she can't fire you.

Determine the Underlying Emotions

Anger is often the secondary emotion that pushes our impulses further into reacting instantaneously. It is very important as a person to be aware of the underlying emotions that might trigger the anger you are feeling. Determining other emotions involved will evidently give you the chance to figure out exactly why you are so angry at those minor mistakes.

The primary emotions include the feeling of rejection, hurt, fear, or sadness. These emotions put together may lead to mixed feelings, interpreted commonly as anger. Most of the anger reaction occurs as an attempt to stop the encroachment of such emotions, to avoid feeling affected by the sources of sadness, fear or hurt.

When you push through problems and avoid the feeling of fear or sadness, you are depriving yourself an essential need for humanity. Anytime you feel hurt, feel everything and continue the journey anyway. Anytime you are sad, acknowledge the reason and work yourself towards finding a reasonable solution, then continue the journey.

Anytime you feel fear, find reasons you feel that emotion. Fear is one of the most important emotions often ignored in order to make ourselves feel like heroes. Being afraid is important in avoiding heartbreaks, failures and even risks that might disrupt a greater part of our happiness as people. So, feel the emotions, act toward them, and never stop chasing what matters until you achieve it.

Be More Aware Of Your Anger Thoughts

Sit quietly and absorb the content of your thoughts. Allow your thoughts to roam around without interrupting the process with conversations or yelling. It is recommended that you stay in a quiet place with less visual distractions in order to practice such form of mindfulness. The level of control you will have on issues concerning your emotions will always depend on the amount of awareness you have for the occurrence of such thoughts.

This aspect of mindfulness should be practiced very often to recognize the progress you are making in handling emotional distractions and aligning your mind unto things that will be highly beneficial to your personal growth. Also, you will be able to recognize the truth behind anger emotions in correlation to the actions of your partner that trigger such emotions.

Evidently, looking at the whole picture of your thoughts will help you determine the most effective mental manipulation that will aid in controlling unwanted feelings. Begin by writing down feelings, and reading them over and over again in order to relate the same feeling to its occurrence in reality.

Perspectives vs. Thoughts and emotions

Since emotions or thoughts are not exclusively the products of external influence, we can easily say that your perception of the environment also plays a big role in the way you feel and interpret things. So, your anger, in general, is **perspective**, not a definite feeling that cannot be changed either by circumstance or people.

On the other hand, understand that your partner might feel a completely different thing even when everything looks the same in the physical. In fact, the reason for your anger may not be that reasonable if your partner doesn't feel the same thing about the same issue. So, it would be wise to also focus on the emotions of your partner and also be able to interpret them.

Also, your expression of how you perceive a particular situation is crucial to the level of understanding your partner will have. Nevertheless, as you grow to understand each other in the relationship, you will begin to think more alike and your anger may not need to be explained.

But you need to work the work of trying to let your partner understand what you are going through in an attempt to reduce the feeling of aloneness in the struggle against the negative emotion.

Accept the Control

Accept that you can be in control of your anger. Accept the facts that you don't necessarily need people to help you control your emotions. Accept that you have the power to allow what should come in or out of your life in general.

 Do not attempt to blame anyone for your feelings even during a particular thought process. Reject the need to involve people when thinking about the causes of your anger. This way you can easily have a clear view of what is going on with you, and the acceptable self-improvement method that can help you reach a definite level of change.

The importance of focusing on you in finding an emotional balance cannot be overemphasized. In the history of human being, the worst distraction many people are yet to deal with is of emotional dependency. The importance of such dependency is only limited to the satisfaction derived from harmonizing with fellow human beings. But when it comes to effective mental and emotional growth, this dependency becomes a stumbling block.

Accepting that you have control or you are responsible for your anger does not mean that everything that is wrong with your emotions is as a result of your actions, but holding on to people's actions and non-actions in determining the stance of your emotion may not allow for the needed perspicacity. Again, self – expression is effectively aided when such focus is being achieved.

The Ownership

Always have the zeal to own your emotions. Your emotions do not have to be determined by what people say you are. Sometimes people will say you are angry, while actually you are just annoyed and out of place.

Most importantly, your emotions are there to communicate to you some details about yourself, your perceptions and strengths. You as a person, you need to understand how you feel, and that becomes only possible when you are able to concentrate on your emotions. And the only way to achieve deeper concentration is when you accept ownership.

Whenever you feel a sudden feeling of irritation, check to see the reasons and how they correlate with the activities you are involved and the whole interpretation of a perception.

How to Control Your Emotions

Your level of emotional control will ultimately determine the level of happiness and satisfaction you derive in your relationship. Your relationship with your Assistant, your colleagues, and even your boss is determined by the amount of control you exercise when you are emotional.

This becomes extremely crucial when it comes to the marriage relationship, where you are expected to act politely and respectfully around one person for the rest of your life. Taking this privilege for granted is as easy as drinking water, but the importance of marriage relationship is as important as the relationship you have to maintain at work. Most of the choices you make in life will depend on this one person, even the job, the time you spend with friends and ultimately where you will relocate after retirement.

As we go deeper into the importance of maintaining the quality of marriage relationship you will also understand deeper the importance of controlling your emotions for the benefit of your spouse, children and the world in general.

Ironically, most of the people that resort to outburst every time they feel angry end up feeling even worst. The unpleasant feeling is carried around, which may result in more act of anger even in the slightest irritation. In the end, nobody is happy.

Depression can be easily induced by repetition of negative thoughts such as anger, sadness, and fear. It is only your thoughts that can have a negative effect on your actions. Your mood is affected, so the way you relate to people is also affected. Unfortunately, bad emotions are easy to adapt to and can become a destructive habit to our entire relationship.

People may stop tolerating you and even your friends may begin to see you as a burden. Part of the control is to never allow your negative emotions or feelings to become a part of you. Once you allow your heart and mind to become a safe haven for bad emotions, positive emotions might not find a place in your life.

Stress and anxiousness are the primary products of worry. When worry becomes an integral part of your life, feeling stressed or anxious might easily become normal. Even though the negative feelings might affect your productivity and acumen, intentional steps need to be taken in order to see the end of the fight. The earlier you begin, the better you do in fighting the negative emotions.

The Reaction

The Reaction is the natural attempt to address an issue that might be detrimental to our emotions. People react to stop other people from hurting them. Even though reactions seem innocent and the best thing to do when attacked with a negative vibe, it ultimately changes your dimension, your feelings, your aim and even your work process.

It is important to note that negative emotions can be a distraction and can make you deviate from other plans in an attempt to put them in check. Focus and time are easily wasted and the result you intend to achieve may be disrupted. But this all changes when you choose to ignore them and keep on moving until you reach a definite goal.

If you don't have to react, you don't have to figure out the reasons for a certain emotion.

If you don't have to react, you don't have to think about your faults, or whether you deserve to be attacked with such negative vibe.

You also don't need to think that this person can finally have power over your reactions since they are able to get your attention and also affect your emotions. Your strength to handle a certain situation too will not be determined since you don't have to fight.

Stop Negative Forecast

Focus on the positivity of the time and stop predicting a negative outcome to things going around you. Responding quickly may render your brain overworked and you have to make sure that everything that comes out of your mouth does not cause destruction. In this case, you need to work fast in filtering any form of attitude or behavior that will tarnish your personality.

Most of the time, people react hastily and regret the outcome. Sometimes what matters is not the fact that you said something or do something wrong, it is the fact that you even reacted in the first place.

On the other hand, negative forecast means assuming this person will act badly since he has acted badly in the past. It is common in marriage when you don't think your spouse cannot improve for good so you continuously label them for their past mistakes. This is detrimental both to your emotional control and to the encouragement they always need in order to change to better people.

You need to have the courage to once again trust that your partner is not going to make the same mistake he or she has made in the past. You need to take the risk to trust them with your life, as a result boosting their self-esteem as people. The worst fear usually doesn't actually happen in real life.

Relating closely with your partner to make sure that you keep the track of their progress, will be beneficial to the amount of emotional control you have over a situation. If you don't act as if someone has already done something bad, you will spread positivity, which your partner will respond by actually making an effort to do the right thing.

It is recommended that you focus your emotions on one thing at a time. You should never ignore your feelings, but make sure you don't allow them to control your thoughts.

Focus On the Problem Instead Of the Person

Emotional attacks or adversities do not come as a Lion or Beast chasing after us. Naturally, the nervous system is built to perceive problems as wild animals threatening to eat our flesh. In order to achieve certain control of the emotions, you need to start perceiving emotional attack or threats differently. You need to stop looking at the people causing the problem and fix your eyes on the problem instead.

If you ever need to solve the problem at hand, do not focus on the person; focus on the reasons for their reactions. Maybe they are intimidated by your effortless success; maybe they feel threatened by the way you are evolving and becoming a better person, even better than they have imagined; maybe they feel the need to give you the negative energy because they still think you are bad at handling emotions, so they have to be defensive.

Once you figure out the reasons for such actions you will begin care less about the people and care more about emotions. Fortunately, most people do the same thing for the same reasons, so you won't need to learn new reasons every day to be able to have control over your emotions.

Once you get used to the reasons, you don't have to ask people to stop acting in some way. Instead, you will focus on controlling the things that can be controlled and letting go of things that may not be relevant to a particular reaction. Once you try to control things you cannot control, you may begin to feel the need for the outburst, since those things may threaten your confidence.

Most problems just occur as part of a life process, so you could just focus on finding solutions instead of blasting blames and yelling at your partner. Another form of reaction that is needed is finding ways you can prevent the repetition of certain bad emotions in your relationship, thus achieving a total peace of mind.

Change the Situation

Change the circumstance by changing your expectancy in a particular situation. For example, if your main aim for working too hard is to achieve perfection so that you can impress people and avoid disappointment, you may encounter anger when after all you did, these people don't seem to care about the quality you have provided.

Changing the purpose for your motivation in pushing further on things can ultimately change your emotions for good. Again, when making decisions upon what to expect, do not expect much from people, they will always disappoint. Let your emotional dependency be about the perfection you provide for yourself and the improvement you achieve a day at a time.

In order to reduce the chances of feeling disappointed when they turn out not to care about what you are doing, your hope should be tied to something else, rather than making an effort to impress all the time. On the other hand, things might go wrong with your plans if you decide to take everything too seriously.

Remember, nothing on earth is perfectly perfect. It is the imperfection that matter to us and you are free to have flaws. Always find easier ways of finishing things and avoid complex combinations in order to get things done faster without the need to feel exposed to stress. Thus, anger or any other negative emotion cannot overcome you.

Choose the Situation

Select the situations your emotions are exposed to, very carefully. For example, there are situations you know that can stir up your anger; or people who are good at making you feel irritated and filled with rage. Avoid situations that have to do with these people as much as possible.

On the other hand, you may not be the kind of person that can handle pressure and deadlines. So instead of waiting for the last day or last minute to finish a task, you could always finish faster in order to reduce the chances of disappointment.

Once you recognize your triggers, you won't have to deal with emotions anymore. Emotional Control starts from how you control the chances of getting emotional as a whole. Same way, if there are people or family members you need to avoid in order to stop feeling irritated, you should strategize a way to stop bumping into them in order to achieve total peace.

Create a Spare Capacity

Firstly, make sure that all your primary needs in life are being met. All the efforts you will make to put your emotions under control may prove futile if your basic needs in life are not met properly. Surprisingly, even though human needs are uniform, everybody has a different priority and of course the different perception of the needs that matter.

Most emotions are counterproductive, and we might experience the same emotion for different reasons. The things we have, and the things we want to have, determine whether we could be strong enough to control a particular emotion or not. Our lacks or abundances determine the level of our vulnerability to external sources of negative emotions.

It is important that you realize your needs; those that are being met, those that you hope will be met when you make some particular effort, and those that you don't really have hope they could be met. Water, shelter, sleep, and food should be provided properly or else your emotions about minor circumstance can never be put under control. Having access to those needs is different from actually meeting those needs. Other needs are ultimately based on individuality and your perceived purpose in life.

Emotional needs are also very important and for an emotion to stay under control, those needs must be met. In fact, once emotional needs are met, self-discipline, maturity, and self-control are easily cultivated. People begin to think more civilized and the animalistic behavior of rage will ultimately reduce even in the marriage relationship.

A person supposed to feel excited to some level every day. Boredom is a bad feeling often ignored and as a result frustration and stagnation may kick in.

People need to expose themselves to situations that will improve their self-esteem. They need to feel like they are growing in status, that they are getting more respect from the people that matter to them.

Everybody wants to feel closely intimate with the people that matter. They want to feel love, have fun and feel the strong energy of friendship even in the marriage relationship. They need to be fed with the sweet talk of affirmation, to be emotionally fulfilled and to see the world getting better in their eyes regardless of the personal challenges they need to go through.

People need to feel like they are among a circle of important individuals in the community. And the circle you find yourself doesn't matter inasmuch as that feeling of importance is there.

Everyone wants to feel like he as a certain control over the things that matter to them. Nobody wants to feel like he or she doesn't have a certain control over his or her life. Everybody deserves and wants control in order to feel emotionally safe.

Whether you are a man or woman, you can't deny the fact that at some point, you crave the attention of other people.

This attention should be quality and must come from the people that matter to you.

Your territory as a person has to be safe, and people that matter to you need to be safe as well. Emotional security needs to be definite, and then all other things could be directed towards you.

When you hear people talk about meaning and purpose in life, the above needs is all they mean. Once you have these things, you will automatically begin to see the value of your life, and you will begin to see clearly the great things you could accomplish with the common talent you have.

Without those needs, you become extremely vulnerable to negativity because you will not feel good about yourself. You may also think your life is meaningless and pointless. So, it is your job as a person to fight for those needs;

to make sure that your relationship provides those needs even as you tend to ignore other fantasies.

Use a Stronger Noggin

Since emotions are not to be ignored or suppressed, you need to find ways to direct and guide every emotion for your benefit. When guided carefully, even negative emotions could be of benefit to our growth and motivations in life. The aim is not to become emotional, but to become gods over the emotions, choosing the right ones as armies in order to win the war against adversaries.

So, instead of reacting physically to emotions, you begin to rationalize and objectify each and every emotion. Only physical attacks require fast response, either for defense or safety. You are required to take your time in order to actually deal with emotions and have actual control over them.

Life is becoming more sophisticated in that your thoughts are today your strongest weapons, and you can achieve whatever you want once you are able to harness them properly. The aim is to force the brain to think even when you feel the strongest emotions taking over you.

Learn From Others

One of the best ways to improve on life skills is the ability to observe and understand how and why other people do things. In fact, it is easier to learn from others how things are being done than going out of our ways creating something new. The challenge is: who are you going to look at? Who is the perfect role model for emotional control?

There is no perfect role model for emotional control. Even your spouse could be that perfect role model. Sometimes you could just witness someone taking control of a particular situation like magic. If they are strangers, you can easily ask them how they are able to manage the irritating situation and took control of the whole result.

If they are your friends or coworkers, you could easily keep quiet and observe them a day at a time. You may want to do more things together with them so you could adapt some of their coping skills, even as you analyze yours and try new ways to put your emotions under control. If your partner has a strong control over emotions, you could also learn from them by attempting to do what they do rightly.

Difficulties and frustrations are easily dealt with when an individual has some amount of emotional intelligence. The questions you could ask are;

Why were they able to keep smiling regardless of the adversaries?

Why didn't they get angry?

And how they exactly keep their cool in the midst of emotional difficulties?

Look Deeper Into the Future

Learn to look deeper into the future by seeing less of the importance of certain emotions. The despair, frustration, depression or anger you feel right now may not matter in the next few days. Your lack or abundance of certain wants may not even matter once you are able to reach a particular height of growth in your relationship.

Look deeper into the near and even the far future and begin to see more hope, above what you can see right now. Let go of the things you can't properly handle, and only focus on things that will actually create some benefits for the present.

Do not allow the intensity of the emotions right now to blind you from the brightness of the future. You should actually believe that now is not all that matters. Anger can make you forget about the future ahead, and dwell in the present, making some bad decisions that may even affect your future as a whole.

You don't need to fire or hurt your spouse when you are dealing with a bad emotion. All you need is some amount of control and you will be able to save the future of your marriage. Even in the place of work, your boss may present to you the hardest emotional puzzle ever known to man that will leave you contemplating whether to insult them, leave or just take the heat. The most important thing to do is to take the heat actually, in order to secure the future, and then leave like a boss.

How to Benefit From Anger

In the real world we are often convinced that getting angry is completely a bad emotion that can easily make us look like bad people once we express them. The truth is; the wildness of the emotion makes it beneficial both for sensibility and growth among human beings. There are things that couldn't have come to life without the aid of the anger emotion. So, instead of consciously avoiding getting angry, you could choose to harness certain anger emotions for the better good.

The self-destructive effect of anger only manifest in people with less control of the emotion and are generally exposed to negativity at a higher rate. In fact, continuous suppression of anger without considering the source and reasons may be significantly self-destructive.

So, redirection becomes an option especially when suppression becomes detrimental. Even in the marriage relationship, anger could be harnessed and directed unto the creation of something big, which could bring a particular growth and harmony among couples.

The aim is to stop treating your anger as something bad and un-showable; to stop feeling like you cannot mention the fact that certain behaviors or occurrences make you unreasonably angry. And this is only possible if you understand the ways you could use anger to provide a physical and emotional breakthrough.

The Negotiating Strategy of Anger

Anger has been long ago used in obtaining things that rightly belonged to people. The legitimacy of anger in this occasion has long ago surpassed the effect of other influences. Anger gets you what you want even when you don't totally deserve that thing.

For example, when negotiating to divide or share something of importance with another person, less sacrifice will be demanded of you when you are perceived to be angry. Thus larger concessions are granted to the person who is angry than the one who shows happiness and harmony.

Controlled anger can be used for negotiation, not the anger that has to do with the outburst, yelling and the use of abusive languages.

Even though being angry might be actually dangerous to the particular negotiation as a whole, anger must be engineered in such a way that people will acknowledge the fact that you have control over your emotions. They need to know that you won't lose your sense but you can go against them strategically due to the emotions of anger you have at that moment.

In all these, make sure your anger is justified by reasons. This will give you power over the intentions and demands of people that matter in the circumstance. When there is no violence or verbal abuse, you can easily get even, and also get the benefit of getting even without losing your respect.

Use Anger to Curb Violence

Use your anger to signal people that an issue needs to be resolved before a particular outburst. Try as much as possible to show how important it is to get these things done to avoid outrage, consequently leading to more violence. This social signal has been used several times in the society among influential people to get people started on some particular work process.

Sometimes the fear of violence becomes the only option for motivation among a group of people. In this case, you use the negative energy to get positive productivity among people. Anger serves as a tool for displaying frustrations and disappointments even in a committed relationship. Your job is to be able to show such emotions elegantly and push people to do better, even as they fight to impress you and attempt to repair the damage that has been made that's making you angry.

Even as you gain more experience with this expression, you should try as much as possible to use it only to fight injustice, incompetence, and laziness among the people that you care about.

Remember, this might not be an ultimate weapon that could work in every circumstance. Be ready to face challenges and oppositions especially in marriage relationships, where everyone is seen as equal. Be wise enough to stay above the negativity, and make sure you use anger to curb violence whenever the strategy could be actually effective.

Use Anger to Gain Greater Acumen

Despite the belief that anger blocks our thoughts and potentials for rationality, recent research proved that anger could provide higher self-insight. Although it is practical that the effect of anger on a particular person depends on how it is handled, it has been made clear that self-insight is definite once the individual allows the emotions of anger to be processed locally in the brain.

You could never discover some of the abilities you have in influencing change or making yourself feel a certain satisfaction until you try anger. In the research, random Russians and Americans were asked about the outcome of a recent outburst. Surprisingly, these people admitted that most of their outburst has brought about a positive outcome, which also involved finding new ways of handling situations and discovering the effect of certain crazy actions on people and their productivity as a whole.

About fifty-five percent of people admit of the benefits of anger to their present state of mind. Thus it has been concluded by the research that even faults could be made right where anger could be applied. For example, you could never realize that your pattern of thoughts about some things will actually work until you take the crazy step of doing things out of anger, bringing your imagination into reality.

On the other hand, you could never know the benefit of some of the things you always think of doing, unless you take a step further in actually doing them. This insight begins when one could actually notice when and why anger invades the emotions. In this case, you receive both your motivation for change through anger, the drive to do something, and can also keep you from doing things that may cause the actual destruction of things that will matter to you in the future.

Use Anger to Grow Your Relationship

Your spouse may not actually know the extent of hurt they are causing unless you express them. One of the ways to express your frustrations about continuous wrongs is through anger. Your aim is not to use violence, but to showcase exactly how you feel when something is being done and to let your spouse know that you are in control your anger. You need to find ways to clearly communicate your feelings without losing control.

In committed relationships, hiding anger is more dangerous than actually showing it. You don't want your partner to think that no wrong has been made. You want a relationship where growth is definite; where each person will accept his or her fault and learn to make corrections without the need to make excuses. When you hide faults as an attempt to hide the fact that you are angry, your partner will continue to do the wrong things, leaving you unhappy and filled with resentment.

Do not ignore the only chance your relationship has for a particular growth. Always put your expression first, and then watch how things will turn out. If your partner doesn't like the way you get angry, then the only option is for them to change for good. Let your treatment and judgment become directly dependent on the level of their improvement. Importantly, your aim should be to look for an actual solution to the problem, to provide suggestions and heads-up for your spouse, so that he or she will follow and become a better person.

Use Anger to Learn Optimism

Normal or neutral emotions have no effect on the way we handle our jobs or how we see things in general. Angry or happy people have more enthusiasm to explore and discover, to create and destroy; and to provide the needed change in a particular work process or industry. The optimistic characteristics of happy people tend to be the same as in angry people, although with a new twist.

According to a research (Lerner et al., 2003), people experiencing anger expect less failure than those experiencing happiness. A happy person will still be anxious that something might still happen that can disrupt their happiness, but an angry person couldn't think of anything worse, so he pushes further and does what has to be done anyway. Anger takes away every fear of failure and builds up the mind to become as flamboyant as possible to reach a given goal.

Pessimism is associated with fear and lack of assurance of the visible future. Fear in general acts as a barricade between the future and the present. Anger overcomes all that and pushes further to seek a forced change.

So, learn to channel your anger unto accomplishment instead of venting and talking about all the bad things that contributed to the emotion. Focus your mind on the things you could accomplish so that you can stay above the feeling. So that the same thing cannot make you angry once you successfully conquer the emotion in question.

Use Anger as a Motivating Force

Going further into using anger as leverage for positive behavior, research studies have been made about the effect of anger on our entire motivations, and how we can use anger to push through both physical and emotional challenges. In some findings, people with certain disabilities tend to find intimidation very arousing in terms of anger, which further pushes them to do something absolutely great despite the difficult route they have to take.

Clearly, anger provides the clear definition of breakthrough, where determination or discipline of any sort is not needed. Anger provides all the motivation to begin and to keep on going on a particular journey. The only work that is demanded of you is the regulation of attitude based on anger and the redirection of emotions towards the desire for performing the greater act that will provide a change in the way things are being executed.

When anger becomes a positive energy, positive actions will be definite and you won't have to worry about the assumed negativity of feeling angry. Goals should be pursued with all zeal and determination; even reward cannot provide the motivation that anger can provide. The aim is to be able to see the benefit of an action first, and when we feel angry, try to still do these things just to get back at the emotion. This is also beneficial as you divert your attention from the person that caused the anger and to the anger itself, using it to achieve something big.

Use Anger as a Cure for Impotence

Although **passivity** is among the forms of anger, being angry actually stimulates you to do something. Instead of being weak and accepting every trash that comes your way, you begin to feel the power and ability to create the actual change you want to see.

In a situation where people you relate with don't see the need to consider your emotions or feelings, crossing over you may not be a problem. But when you create a particular outburst due to anger even for once, you realize that you have the ability to actually earn respect without the need to accept every trash that comes your way.

Not just in your marriage relationship, you need to acknowledge the fact that the world is cruel and you need to have a certain power in order to overcome this cruelty. Acceptance is no more charming and adorable. Accepting everything only makes you a fool for other people, and your emotions could easily be used as a playground for foul-filled games.

In your relationship with people, yourself, health, personal fitness, finance, job and friendship, you need to be adequate enough to deal with challenges as they show themselves. Use the anger instantaneously to do that thing you've been thinking about doing all this while, thus your reaction will not be reckless but a planned action, which only needed a motivation to come to life.

You will suddenly achieve a boost in confidence, and all the lowly frustrations and conflicts will be put to check. So, confront that situation you've been avoiding and create the change that you are the only person can create. Whenever you feel some doubt, try to remember the vivid scenario that made you angry, replay it on your mind and push even further.

Use Anger as a Protection

At some point in life, threats do not make you afraid; threats make you irritated and angry. The only option left when the threat is presented is to adapt or survive. Anger helps you to fight further for survival, instead of the adoption of discomfort.

On the other hand, anger helps you to implement the necessary defensive tactics against adversaries. The impossible could be accomplished when anger is applied as a driving force. You automatically feel the power to be able to stop any person or character that stands as a stumbling block in your journey to happiness and satisfaction. And instead of feeling sorry after the "did" has been done, you will push further to create even a better platform for your ideologies to stick.

Anger makes you want to fight to the death until you make things right. The aim is not to use anger to fight everything worth fighting; the aim is to make yourself less of a victim by taking action that can turn you into a victor. Specifically, use anger to defend and protect your interests, not to manipulate.

Use Anger to Interact

Anger is the strongest form of interaction often ignored by people. The best way to tell someone how alienated, unexcited, dissatisfied and unfulfilled you are is the expression of the anger emotion. Verbal expression of anger when regulated could be a strong tool for communicating feelings vividly to a particular audience. It makes the inexpressible once again expressible.

Apart from the simple expression, it gets people to actually act toward calming you down, which mean doing things the right way. When something needs correction, and the person involved is not actually responsive in making sure the correction has been made, frustration could be easily expressed to push them further unto doing the impossible.

Before you resort to verbal expression, have a small dialogue with yourself about the effect and the outcome of the things you are about to say. Make sure you make a definite assessment of the way people are going to perceive the whole emotion, compared to the instant benefit that will be provided. In this case, self-dialogue could bring more awareness of the effect of anger and how different forms of anger could be directed differently to interact with other humans.

Use Anger to Develop New Habit

Anger makes you more competent even in your personal life. Disappointment as a result of lack of good performance might bring about a strong anger. Use that feeling to develop habits that could actually change the way you do things. Take the opportunity to actually change something in your life.

Are afraid to try something new? Use the anger emotion as a motivation to push through. Allow yourself to be disturbed by your stagnancy, feel the pain and anger, and then take action anyway. Do not miss the opportunity of experiencing a new feeling by actually heading towards a new direction.

Dealing with Angry Spouse

Despite the said benefit of controlled anger, uncontrolled anger can destroy your relationship in a minute. It is your job as a partner to control the anger of your spouse, to make sure they don't do anything stupid, which they will later regret. The reasons for anger sometimes may not justify an outburst, in that all anger needs to be controlled and regulated.

The harm of outburst is always the same: regrets. Your response to their outbursts is very important as an attempt to save your marriage and happiness as a whole. The way you respond to an angry spouse may either make or break your relationship. It is something you need to keep in mind, even as you make a balanced analogy of your weaknesses and how you can improve to reduce negative outbursts in your marriage.

First of all, empathy is a strong weapon for building intimacy and ultimately rekindling the lost passion of a relationship. In the case of anger, empathy plays a very important role in calming individuals down. It is very important that they feel understood whenever they are angry, to allow them to talk and be as emotional as possible. Thus you will have the opportunity to stay in control regardless of their negativity.

Use the Distraction Diffusion Technique

Distract your spouse from the reason of their frustrations, and unto something really interesting. Let the focus be genuine and for a particular time.

Rumination of anger is only possible when the person continues to pay attention to the factors that are responsible for the bad feeling. But distraction changes everything, where the person will be able to take a timeout. Subconsciously, this person will calm down, and also realize the essence of sanity in handling even the most sensitive situations.

One of the most effective forms of distraction is laughter. First of all, never ever use sarcasm to calm an angry person. Sarcasm is ridicule, inasmuch as an angry person is concerned, and could even make them feel worse.

Make a funny joke or show them a funny video that they can't resist laughing. Expose them to situations that will make them light up, and then immediately ask them if they want to talk about the bad feeling.

Passive or assertive anger can easily be circumvented using the distraction diffusion technique. You should know the extent of anger in order to determine the kind of distraction that could actually work for the moment. Active anger may need more effort and time. So, you need to be patient with the slowness of their response to the elements of distraction.

Apologize and Find an Instant Solution

When someone is already angry, try as much as possible not to use excuses to calm them down, it will only get worse. Try to make them feel like you have understood the reasons for their anger and actually apologize for the mistake. Do not defend your actions immediately in order to get hold of the situation. Except if the context of feeling angry is totally wrong, do not try to make yourself look better until they are already calm.

Also, in the process of apologizing, ask them for the ways they think the issue could be resolved and listen to them attentively. To make what they say look even more important, look for a pen and a paper and write everything down as they say it.

The aim here is to make sure the storm is calmed so that you will get the opportunity to rebuild what was already shattered, and to tell your own part of the story when you know you have their full attention. An apology is the essence of growth in the relationship. Apologizing when they are hurt will make them even apologize for the way they acted in the first place.

Identify the Cause of Anger

Sometimes the real cause of anger is not the situation at hand. It could be the combination of several emotions put together for a particular period of time. Make sure you recognize and determine the causes in order to have ideas on how to avoid future occurrence of outbursts.

Ask proper questions and observe both their body language and verbal emphasis. If the emphasis is about deprivation, find out exactly why they feel deprived. If it's about frustration, make sure you put everything in place to figure out exactly the source of his or her frustration.

In all these, do not interrupt the person. Always encourage them to keep on talking as you actively listen and even ask for more explanation when they are quiet. The aim is to see things from their point of view, to put your legs in their shoes so that you will know exactly what to do and what not to do, to improve your relationship. Active listening cannot be overemphasized in this case.

And when responding to their questions or accusations, make sure you are calm and slow. Lower your voice as you take every point, to make yourself clear. Your body language should not be threatening, and not indicting either. Do everything you can to assure them that relaxing will not make them look weak again. Use the power of empathy, in this case, to also communicate about their feelings and emotions.

Be specific when making a point and always use real-life situations when making references. You should focus on finding a solution and stay away from judgmental statements. Respect them and show that you could be a champion for them once again. Ask them exactly how they want to be treated, and do the exact things they say.

Create an Emotional Distance

Realize when you are not responsible for your spouse's anger. Realize when all you have to do is to listen, and you will be alright. It's your job to first understand the reason why someone is angry before you take any particular action in calming them down. So, do not get upset by the situation yet. Find ways to help them cope with the emotions even as you create a distance between feeling what they are feeling and actually causing the feeling.

Do not be sorry for the way your spouse's boss treats him or her. Your job is to make them feel good, not to take the blame. When they are calm you can suggest to them some wise ways to handle the emotions, or even the person, without the need to bring back the negative energy home.

Negative feelings are easily transmitted since people feel the need to relate their bad feeling so they won't be the only ones' experiencing them. On the other hand, some people may actually use anger to make themselves feel good; and that means making people feel even worse. The best solution is to provide distance between the occurrence of each emotion in the other person and your response.

This also brings about the importance of boundaries even in committed relationships. And if you are the cause of the emotion, do not shy away from the responsibility of making the person feel good again, even when it means making them hope that you could do better next time.

Do Not Respond With Anger

In whatever situation, do not respond to anger with anger. The beginning of every fight is when both parties are angry at each other and nobody resorts to calmness. They might be wrong but if you are still calm, you should maintain that state of mind until everything is over. After the yelling and all the troubling, you can talk to them about how wrong they handled the situation.

Even when you feel like you are under attack, only use protective-verbalism to make sure you don't get hurt physically or even emotionally. Let your intelligence lead the way to a solution. Let calmness overcome every crazy responses and emotion.

Deep breathing, in this case, is very important. Counting from **one** to **ten** before responding to an angry statement might help in giving out a great speech that will calm the person down. Be the one in control of emotions. Relax and let nature takes its course in turning negative situations into blessings.

Also, it is only wise to excuse yourself when you feel like you can't take the intensity of the interaction anymore. It is better to walk out of the conversation than to actually raise voices with your partner or anybody else.

Stay Safe

Actually, it doesn't matter whether you are dealing with a man or woman. Angry people could be very dangerous at times. If you have the chance, leave the room for them once they begin to show signs of violence.

Fear or anger could be mixed together in this case. Follow the fear emotion and save yourself the need to battle with violence or emotional abuse.

In terms of controlling anger in other people, you need to be able to trust your judgment. Trust that everything you do from now will depend on your feelings. Know when the person is getting out of control and look for a safe zone.

Conclusion

Managing anger both in yourself and other people is very important in setting great examples for your spouse to follow. Calming down even when you supposed to be angry will make them rethink their outburst and actually come down to your level. The purpose should not only be to manage your anger but to inspire others to manage the emotions effectively. Transformation is only possible when such example is given.

Building positive relationship is very crucial to your image as a person. The respect you get in the outside world reflects to the way you are going to be treated in your own home, and vice versa. You should be able to control the anger emotions in order to influence positivity in your marriage relationship. This way you will be exposed to happiness and understanding, and every mistake will be taken as an opportunity for growth. There will be less stress in trying to hide or express your emotions because you know someone significant does understand the reasons you do things.

Your response to anger is also very important to the whole process of change and growth in relationship. Aggressiveness is only determined by the way you respond to situations, not how you feel or what you are thinking. You should response to someone else's anger passively until you find a strong ground where you can infuse or showcase positive energy in order to create a particular change. The aim is to be seen as the mediator, to create the change and to do less in igniting anger and resentment.

Other Books by the Same Author

1. 100 Ways to Cultivate Intimacy in Your Marriage: How to Improve Communication, Build Trust and Rekindle Love

2. 200 Ways to Seduce Your Husband: How to Boost Your Marriage Libido and Actually Enjoy Sex: A Couple's Intimacy Guide

3. 232 Questions for Couples: Romantic Relationship Conversation Starters for Connecting, Building Trust, and Emotional Intimacy

4. Communication in Marriage: How to Communicate Effectively With Your Spouse, Build Trust and Rekindle Love

Printed in Great Britain
by Amazon